How to personalize this book for your Dear Son!

Tools needed: (all are available at a scrapbook supply store and/or craft store)
- Acid-free glue stick
- Photo mounting squares/tape
- Scissors or photo trimmer
- Fine point writing pen (acid-free, light-fast, waterproof, fade-proof, smear-proof and non-bleeding)
- Acid-free paper for writing additional notes/letters

Dear Friends,

We created this book to be a precious keepsake for sons of all ages. Given that some of us are "craftier" than others, we designed it so you can add as much or as little personalization as you'd like. Take a look at some of the ways you can add your own special touch...

Customize the cover photo

Slip out the cover insert and paste your special photo in the indicated area. Instantly, you transform this book into something especially for YOUR son!

Cover personalized with photo

Paste your photos over ours!

One of the easiest ways to make this book your own is to gather your favorite family photos and paste them over the ones we show. Some spaces are a traditional 4 x 6 size; others are circular or sub-sized. For the cleanest cuts, you would want to use a photo trimmer (see above).

Page personalized with photos and memorabilia

Tuck a heartfelt message into the vellum envelopes on pgs. 18 and 27

What are your hopes and dreams for your son? How much do you cherish him? Tell him in your own words and place your note in one of two special envelopes.

Page personalized with photo, fortune, hand writing and letter in pocket

Affix to pages mementos of special memories, i.e., ticket stubs, postcards, etc.

Did you and your son share a special trip? Attend an event together? A memento of such an experience can be a nice addition to a page.

Page personalized with photo and hand writing

Handwrite your own thoughts or advice on pg. 35

What words of wisdom would you like to share with your son? You can certainly add your anecdotes to any page. We have, however, built in a special page for "mom's advice."

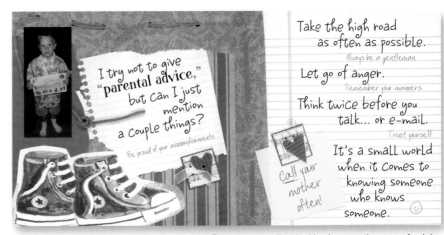

Page personalized with photo and notes of advice

Dear Son

a message of Love

by
Marianne Richmond

Dear Son
a message of Love

Library of Congress Control Number: 2005907884

© 2006 by Marianne Richmond Studios, Inc.

A special thanks to the creative companies whose papers we incorporated into our designs: daisyd's, Karen Foster Design, Design Originials, Making Memories©, K&Company LLC, C.R. Gibson, Masterpiece Studios.

Marianne Richmond Studios, Inc.
420 N. 5th Street, Suite 840
Minneapolis, MN 55401
www.mariannerichmond.com

ISBN 09770000-7-9

Illustrations by Marianne Richmond

Book design by Sara Dare Biscan

Printed in China

First Printing

Dear _____

_____

_____

_____

_____

Love,

_____

Dear Son,

You are my beloved boy.

Daring & Delightful.

FAST BREAK!

ENERGETIC

CURIOUS

I Love this Game!

FUNNY

How Lucky I am
to have

thE
gIft
of
you

in my Life.

I love watching you tackle the world with enthusiasm,

a willingness to get down and dirty and with a bit of "boy craziness."

time

after

time,

> "Families are like fudge: mostly sweet with a few nuts."
>
> *Author unknown*

a chip off the old block

Even though we know I don't often do **OR** say the right thing. Just know I'm giving it my all for your journey.

thelastword

I'm amazed by how smart and creative

and capable you are.

dreams
&ideas

⭐ How your mind is filled with so many awesome dreams and ideas.

Do you know how **incredible** you are?

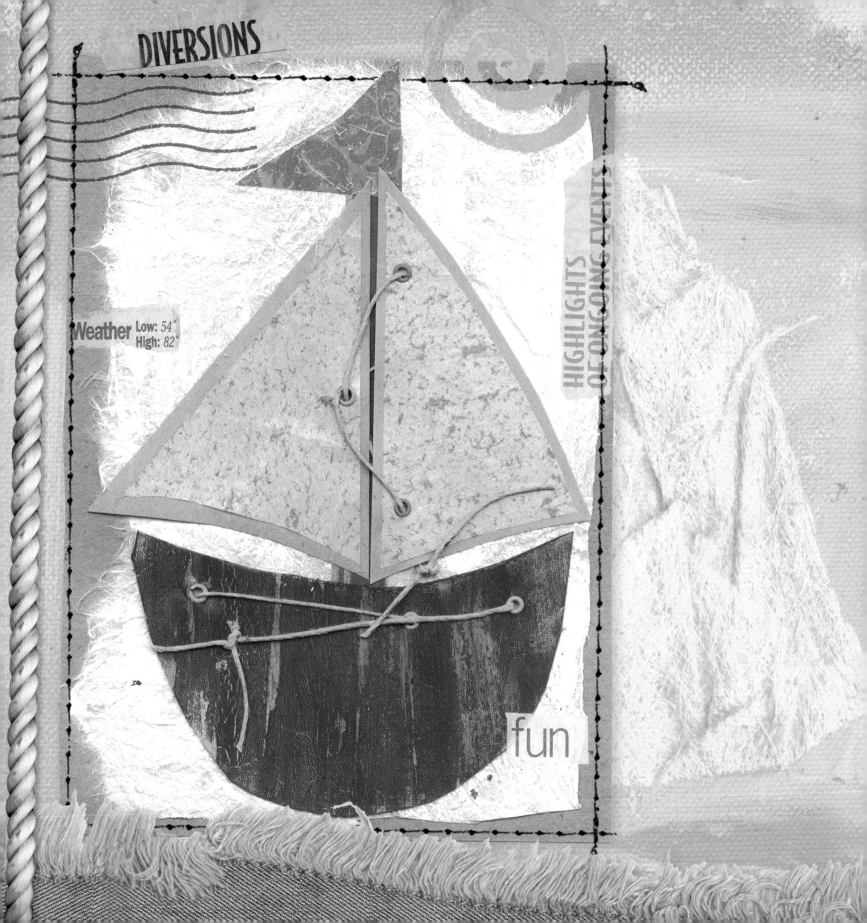

Weather Low: 54°
High: 82°

HIGHLIGHTS OF ONGOING EVENTS

fun

I wish for you... wonderful
Life **adventures**,

forever
kind
of
friendships

and **opportunities** to pursue
your greatest passions.

HUG

Though boys are known for being "**tough guys**," I wish for people to be kind to your heart.

AND to realize that strong on the outside doesn't mean unbreakable on the inside.

While I can't promise you a trouble-free journey,

I can tell you that **strength** is born amidst the struggles and disappointments.

Cherish The Moments

creating the future

preserving the past

My heart aches when I see you sad or hurting.

PROTECTION

life's journey

wishes for you...

prayers

dreams

I don't know if
you know how often
I pray for you...
for your guidance and
wisdom
and protection.

I know you think I'm "too much" sometimes.

Too protective, too sappy AND too affectionate.

BUT, I also know, deep down, you probably like it.

I want so much the B E S T for you, and it's hard for me to let go sometimes.

To let you choose, explore, experience, and, at times, regret.

My LOVE for you is just that great.

I see part
of my job
is to teach
you to be

GOOD VALUES

a thoughtful, well-mannered young man.

And to treat women with **respect** and **kindness.** You just might have a "Lady" in your Life someday.

(yikes!)

Mother knows best

I'm so

PROUD

of you for
who you are.
I want you to feel
proud of you, too.

Take the high road
as often as possible.

Let go of anger.

Think twice before you
talk... or send e-mail.

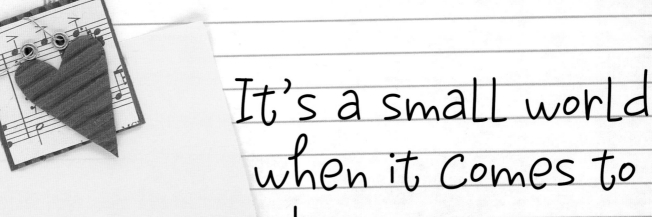

It's a small world
when it comes to
knowing someone
who knows
someone.

And when
you think

?

see eye-to-eye

COMFORT

I can't possibly
understand,

I'M HOME

welcome

I
hope
you
realize
that
I
just

might.

I Love
you **more** than
words can ever say.
From head-to-toe tip,
you are my

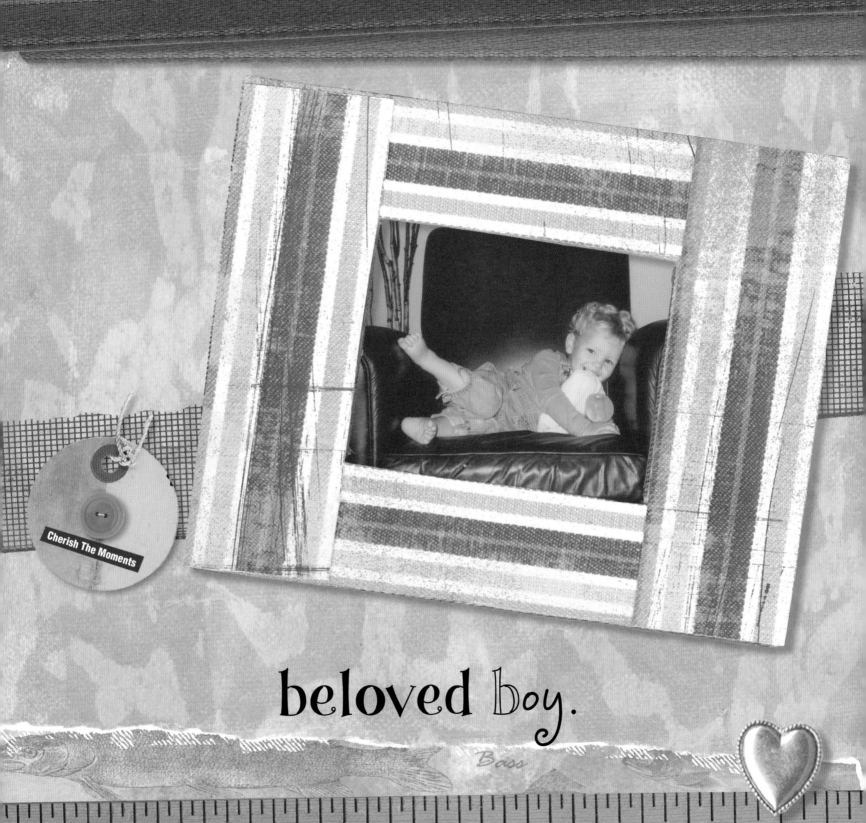

Cherish The Moments

beloved boy.

Bass